Worship through Novels

Short Stories and Fairy Tales

Regan Kim

Copyright © 2021 Regan Kim

WORSHIP THROUGH NOVELS

Contents

Foreword

Worship Through Novels is a book that digs for gems in the desert. It is a unique attempt to find Biblical lessons from the characters, dialogues, events, and plots of many well-known novels and apply them to the Christian life.

It is by no means easy to find Biblical values in a novel by connecting the story with the Bible. By doing so, the Biblical values presented to the reader will be enriched with spiritual food, no matter what novels they read.

Regan Kim is a spiritual soldier who establishes the values of the Kingdom of God by viewing everything that happens in the world from a Biblical point of view.

Regan refers to it as *Worship Through Novels*, naming the Biblical lessons mined from the novel; it shows how to live as worshipers in your life by practising the Scripture "present your bodies as holy living sacrifices". (Romans 12:2)

It is a valuable model for believers whose faith and everyday life are separate. I would like to highly recommend reading this book that challenges you to try the same thing in your life. I applaud him for his amazing feat.

Nam Woo-Taek,
Senior Pastor of Han-Ou-Ri Presbyterian Church

Introduction

Worship through Novels and Christian Life

My first language is Korean; nevertheless, I wanted to publish this book in English because the universal language provides more opportunities to reach people worldwide. For this book, I didn't hesitate to use the easy English that I was used to, and I believe plain English will bring the messages closer to non-native readers like myself.

Worship Through Novels is not intended to convey literary knowledge or build culture. It has only one purpose; it is to worship Jesus through fiction.

When reading fiction, readers are confronted with many different characters and situations. When a Believer starts identifying with one of the characters, they start practising a Christian life in reality, by examining the life of the character they identify with, and how that life aligns with their faith, or not.

John 10:27 NIV says, "My sheep listen to my voice; I know them, and they follow me."

The Christian life is about following Jesus. It is not given for free; it requires training. Remember that Jesus' disciples were trained for three years. First of all, it is essential to practise setting up the Biblical point of view, no matter what you do.

If you read stories from a worldly perspective, Jesus is invisible because the world blindfolds your eyes. Isaiah 45:15 NIV says, "Truly you are a God who has been hiding himself, the God and Saviour of Israel." However, when you read a novel with a Biblical perspective, even in a non-Christian story, you can find Jesus hidden in the fictional story.

Romans 12:1 NIV says: "Therefore, I urge you, brothers and sisters, in view of God's mercy, to offer your bodies as a living sacrifice, holy and pleasing to God—this is your true and proper worship."

Paul, the apostle, urges the church to worship God by offering daily life as a living sacrifice.

Once you read through my reviews, I am sure you'll experience how valuable and beneficial it is to worship through fictional stories. This book also includes memorable quotes from each story, so readers can catch where those Biblical lessons were obtained.

Experiencing a variety of lives through fiction will give you a valuable chance to practice the life of living sacrifice. *Worship Through Novels* will be a training ground for you to have a Jesus-centred point of view under any circumstances.

We live novel-like lives, and fiction is like a laboratory of real life. *Worship Through Novels* will guide you to *Worship Through your Lives*.

Regan Kim

Part A

Novels

Chapter 1 -
Don Quixote

Overview

Although God has given it to you, is there any dream you're just sitting on? When you read *Don Quixote*, you may remember dreams that you have long forgotten.

This extraordinary book was published in 1605 by Miguel de Cervantes Saavedra, a Spanish writer. (The book review covers the first part of it.)

The protagonist is a nobleman of around 50 years of age from the village of La Mancha. He spent most of his time reading books of chivalry and finally became mentally obsessed with the idea of himself as a knight. He named himself Don Quixote of La Mancha, dressed as a knight and equipped with a weapon.

The self-proclaimed knight-errant went on an adventure to actualise chivalry against injustice and win the love of Dulcinea, his imaginary princess. His first journey ended in three days. As soon as he returned home, the clergyman and barber took all the chivalry books out of his library and burned them because they thought those books made Don Quixote crazy.

Don Quixote set off his second adventure along with his new attendant, Sancho Panza. The self-declared knight promised to let Sancho, a farm labourer, become governor of an island.

Don Quixote did not stop causing various bizarre events the whole time during the ridiculous adventure. He attacked thirty-four windmills, falsely believing those were giants. The wacky protagonist rushed to a herd of sheep, mistaking them for enemies, and he tried to save prisoners from guards claiming they were innocent. Also, he performed penance in the mountains to win Dulcinea's love.

Worried about Don Quixote, the cleric and barber finally picked him up on an oxen cart and brought him home.

The first part of the book ends like this. In the second part, Don Quixote realises that he is not a knight-errant and dies in despair. Needless to say, Don Quixote suffers from severe mental health issues; nevertheless, readers are attracted to him because of his challenge and courage; he never hesitates to take an adventure, getting out of the comfort zone.

Biblical Lessons

Anyone trying to achieve their dream is likely to be considered reckless. Paul, the apostle, was filled with dreams to spread the Gospel but was mocked as a crazy person.

That was when Paul spoke in his defence against the accusations made by the Jewish leaders. Festus, the Roman governor who was listening, suddenly shouted, "Paul, you are insane. Too much study has made you crazy!" (Acts 26:24 NLT)

When it comes to dreams, there will be no book as full of dreams as the Bible. Heaven and earth were created from God's dream of building up His kingdom, and Jesus' work of redemption is also being led by God's vision of fulfilling a new heaven and a new earth. (Revelation 21:1)

The Bible also tells us that God plants His vision in Christians' hearts and allows them to participate in His ministry.

"For God is working in you, giving you the desire and the power to do what pleases him." (Philippians 2:13 NLT)

In this novel, Don Quixote's team was a mixed bag by worldly standards. The knight lacked fighting skill, and his helmet was made of a basin. His horse, Rocinante, was skinny, and Sancho Panza used to be a farm-worker.

But Don Quixote was so proud that he was a knight-errant anyway. He introduced himself to a troop of more than two hundred men:

"I, sirs, am a knight-errant whose calling is that of arms, and whose profession is to protect those who require protection, and give help to such as stand in need of it." (Chapter 27, P628)

Jesus' disciples were no different either. Just before Jesus ascended to heaven, He commanded them to go to all nations to make disciples (Matthew 28:19) and to be His witnesses to the ends of the earth (Acts 1:8).

The first disciples, who received the order back then, were only eleven simple men, including un-schooled fishermen. (Matthew 28:19; Acts 4:13)

However, when the Holy Spirit later came down upon one hundred twenty disciples, they were filled with God's dream. Acts 2:17 NIV says, "In the last days, God says, I will pour out my Spirit on all people. Your sons and daughters will prophesy, your young men will see visions, your old men will dream dreams."

Since then, Jesus' followers began to spread the Gospel confidently and courageously and eventually evangelised even the Roman empire, which ruled the world at that time.

And, what is it going on now with Jesus' command to preach the Gospel to all nations? Amazingly, the church is running toward the final list of unreached races. Therefore, even if the world laughs at them, Christians should not give up on challenges when God gives them dreams.

The difference between Followers of Christ and Don Quixote is that Don Quixote's dreams were his own selfish dreams of grandeur. Whereas Christians are not following a silly, selfish dream but are following the commands of Jesus to tell the good news of His death and resurrection, and how that gives us eternal life through faith in Him. When God gives you a dream or vision for your future, you can be courageous like Don Quixote, but you will know that God backs it up.

Don Quixote can be a breakthrough in readers' blocked minds if they feel frustrated by the wall of common sense that limits their dreams.

Memorable Quotes

*Reference Book: Miguel De Cervantes. (1605). *Don Quixote*. translated by John Ormsby. (Evergreen Classics). Kindle E-Book.

- o Part 1, Chapter 1, P16 (knight-errant's love)
  So then, his armour being furbished, his morion turned into a helmet, his hack christened, and he himself confirmed, he came to the conclusion that nothing more was needed now but to look out for a lady to be in love with; for a knight-errant without love was like a tree without leaves or fruit, or a body without a soul.

o Part 1, Chapter 8, P50 (windmills)

"What giants?" said Sancho Panza. "Those thou seest there," answered his master, "with the long arms, and some have them nearly two leagues long." "Look, your worship," said Sancho; "what we see there are not giants but windmills, and what seem to be their arms are the sails that turned by the wind make the millstone go."

But as he drove his lance-point into the sail the wind whirled it round with such force that it shivered the lance to pieces, sweeping with it horse and rider, who went rolling over on the plain, in a sorry condition.

o Part 1, Chapter 27, P628 (knight-errant's profession)

With this permission Don Quixote went on to say, "I, sirs, am a knight-errant whose calling is that of arms, and whose profession is to protect those who require protection, and give help to such as stand in need of it."

- o Part 2, Chapter 74, P922 (doctor's opinion)

  The doctor's opinion was that melancholy and depression were bringing him to his end.

- o Part 2, Chapter 74, P926 (death of Don Quixote)

  At last, Don Quixote's end came, after he had received all the sacraments and had in full and forcible terms expressed his detestation of books of chivalry. The notary was there at the time, and he said that in no book of chivalry had he ever read of any knight-errant dying in his bed so calmly and so like a Christian as Don Quixote, who amid the tears and lamentations of all present yielded up his spirit, that is to say died.

Chapter 2 -
The Old Man and The Sea

Overview

If you are going through a dark tunnel in your life, pick up this book and open the first page. You will soon immerse yourself in all the stories of Santiago's misfortune, struggle, Pyrrhic victory, and finally, you will see the light of hope coming from Jeremiah 29:11.

"For I know the plans I have for you," says the Lord. "They are plans for good and not for disaster, to give you a future and a hope. (NLT)

The Old Man and The Sea was published in 1952 by Ernest Miller Hemingway, an American novelist and the 1954 Nobel Prize winner in Literature.

Santiago, the main character, was an old Cuban fisherman. He had gone eighty-four days without catching a fish, but eventually, he was able to hook a giant marlin far in the ocean. He fought tooth and nail to catch the fish. It had been as many as three days until Santiago killed it with a harpoon.

But the joy wore off quickly. A shark smelled the dead fish's blood and chased after it. Santiago bent over backwards to resist the shark and finally killed it.

The veteran had a hunch of another shark attack at hand. He pulled himself together and said firmly, "But man is not made for defeat. A man can be destroyed but not defeated."

Sure enough, two sharks and, next, more sharks carried out a raid. Santiago could no longer do anything to defend his trophy, and the marlin ended up reduced to only its backbone. He managed to get to the port with the leftover bones hanging next to the skiff.

Before this event, Santiago used to have a boy assistant named Manolin. As the old man hadn't caught anything for many days, the boy's parents had him work on another boat. The old man missed Manolin the whole time he worked alone in the sea.

Manolin began to cry when he saw the returnee's hands hurt badly. The boy promised to go with him next time.

Hemingway wrote the last scene like this: He was still sleeping on his face, and the boy was sitting by him watching him. The old man was dreaming about the lions.

Biblical Lessons

In this story, Santiago's heart for the marlin is not hostile at all. As a fisherman, he tried to catch it, and the fish escaped to the end. The old man felt brotherhood for the marlin doing his best. He pitied the resisting fish, thinking, 'I wish I could feed the fish.'

But Santiago had to kill the marlin anyway. He said, "Fish, I love you and respect you very much. But I will kill you before this day ends."

After catching the fish, he thought he had killed his brother, and he felt guilty. He asked himself, "If you love him, it is not a sin to kill him. Or is it more?"

On the contrary, the fisherman treated sharks differently. After killing the first shark, Santiago said, "I killed him in self-defence. And I killed him well." For him, sharks were just predators and depredators.

His attitude toward sharks is in line with the Bible's view of Satan.

Jesus said, "Love your enemies" (Matthew 5:44 NIV), but that does not apply to Satan. 1 John 3:8

NIV says, "The devil has been sinning from the beginning." He's not a sinner like us but sin itself.

As a result, the sharks beat Santiago. This ending implies the fact that no one can defeat sin with his own strength.

Think about Adam. He was perfect but knocked down by sin. So, how can all his descendants overcome evil when they are born sinful?

People often say, "I can do everything," but that's not true. The truth is, "I can do everything through Christ, who gives me strength." (Philippians 4:13 NLT)

Throughout the story, the old man had dreams about lions which he'd seen on the beaches of Africa in earlier sea adventures of his younger years. The image of the lions in Santiago's dreams is reminiscent of Jesus in the Bible. Christ Jesus is called the Lion of the tribe of Judah in Revelation 5:5. One hopes Santiago's dream about lions would be a spiritual opportunity to lead him to Jesus.

Let's think about one more thing. Santiago missed Manolin while he fought alone in the sea, but he will never be alone again because the boy promised to go with the old man.

In the future, nothing will beat their dream team. For the two will unite in trusting each other and be together. So too, when we trust Jesus, the Lion of the tribe of Judah, He has promised He will always be with us. Together with Jesus, we are the ultimate dream team!

Memorable Quotes

*Reference Book: Ernest Hemingway. (1952). *The Old Man and The Sea.* (Canada: Produced by Al Haines. 2012). Kindle E-Book.

- o P32 (Fish, I love you)

  "Fish," he said, "I love you and respect you very much. But I will kill you dead before this day ends."

- o P63 (Man is not made for defeat)

  It was too good to last, he thought. I wish it had been a dream now and that I had never hooked the fish and was alone in bed on the newspapers.

  "But man is not made for defeat," he said. "A man can be destroyed but not defeated."

- ○ P64 (sin)

  Perhaps it was a sin to kill the fish. I suppose it was even though I did it to keep me alive and feed many people. But then, everything is a sin.

  You were born to be a fisherman as the fish was born to be a fish. You loved him when he was alive, and you loved him after. If you love him, it is not a sin to kill him. Or is it more?

- ○ P64 (sharks)

  But you enjoyed killing the dentuso*, he thought. He lives on the live fish as you do. He is not a scavenger nor just a moving appetite as some sharks are.

  He is beautiful and noble and knows no fear of anything. "I killed him in self-defence," the old man said aloud. "And I killed him well."

  *Dentuso is the nickname for the kind of shark that attacked. It is Spanish for "big toothed" and used mostly for the mackerel shark.

o   P75-76 (They beat me)
"They beat me, Manolin," he said. "They truly beat me." "He didn't beat you. Not the fish." "No. Truly. It was afterwards."

o   P78 (dreaming about the lions)
Up the road, in his shack, the old man was sleeping again. He was still sleeping on his face and the boy was sitting by him watching him. The old man was dreaming about the lions.

Chapter 3 - Demian

Overview

This book was published in 1919 by Hermann Karl Hesse, a German-Swiss novelist and 1946 Nobel Prize winner in Literature. Here's the summary.

Emil Sinclair grew up in the care of his parents. For him, the world meant love, example and school. In his parents' world, there was a straight path to a safe and bright future.

His smooth life was interrupted by Franz Kromer, a school bully. Max Demian, a new transfer student, saved Sinclair from Kromer. He sorted out the bullying at once in a mysterious way.

Demian was different from ordinary students. His views on good and evil were peculiar. For example, he thought Cain was a good fellow even though he killed Abel. He insisted that God's mark on Cain (see Genesis 4:15) was not for punishment but a sign of Cain's power.

Sinclair transferred to a boarding school, where he was reduced to an outsider. He indulged in alcohol in the name of seeking his inner self. One day, Sinclair had a dream about a bird of prey with a hawk's head, working to escape from a giant egg. He painted it and sent it to Demian. The reply from Demian was as follows:

"The bird fights its way out of the egg. The egg is the world. Whoever will be born must destroy a world. The bird flies to god. The name of the god is Abraxas."

The opportunity to learn about Abraxas came to Sinclair. He stumbled upon organist Pistorius, an advocate for Abraxas, and heard about Abraxas from him. Pistorius had studied theology but had lost his faith in the Christian God.

When the war between Germany and Russia finally broke out, Demian fought as a lieutenant, and Sinclair later joined the battle. After a bomb went off nearby Sinclair, he was put in a makeshift ward.

Unexpectedly, he found Demian next to him, but Demian was gone when he woke up. Sinclair soon realised that he completely resembled Demian.

Biblical Lessons

What do you say about this novel? As you see, *Demian* is a religious novel. In particular, it opposes Christianity, saying that God represents only the bright side of the world.

This novel introduces their god called Abraxas, a god and devil accepting both the bright and dark worlds.

According to Abraxas advocates, revealing a sinful nature was part of self-realisation.

They don't suppress anything at all, whether it is good or evil, including sexual desire.

In the preface titled "The Story of Emil Sinclair's Youth", Hermann Hesse wrote like this; "I wanted only to try to live in obedience to the promptings which came from my true self. Why was that so very difficult?"

For Abraxas's followers, the laws and commandments in the Bible were only eggs for birds to destroy.

Of course, a bird has to destroy its egg to fly, which is an obvious truth. However, Abraxas is the wrong destination. Who on earth is Abraxas? The Bible reveals the true identity. He is none other than Satan that showed up in Genesis 3.

The devil tempted Adam and Eve to eat the fruit of knowledge of good and evil. What did Satan say at that time? "God knows that your eyes will be opened as soon as you eat it, and you will be like God, knowing both good and evil." (Genesis 3:5 NLT)

The story that a bird breaks its egg to fly to Abraxas is the same as the fall of Adam and Eve, who plummeted into depravity.

Let's examine one controversial issue. The novel has the following statements that glamorise the meaning of World War I:

Sinclair, on the battlefield, saw a giant bird was destroying its egg. The egg was the world, so the world had to go to ruin.

Something, a new order of humanity, was in the process of forming.

Soldiers' murderous and bloody work was an expression of their inner being to be born anew.

Hermann Hesse is known as an anti-war pacifist; even so, how come he justified World War 1?

Thomas Mann (1875-1955), a German novelist, appraised *Demian* like this:

"*Demian*…moved an entire young generation with grateful delight.

"This severely insightful author must be a messiah from their midst."

Would it be the reason? Did the author wish to restore the pride and hope of German youth who were depressed by the defeat of World War I?

Hermann Hesse didn't clearly answer this contradiction, so today's readers are only confused about it.

Now, it's time to wrap up. Suppose you and I, as Christian readers, received the bird's picture from Sinclair instead of Demian. How would we respond to this?

Two Bible verses come to mind. The first is Psalm 51:5 NLT. "For I was born a sinner- yes, from the moment my mother conceived me."

The egg that a bird has to break is, after all, the sinful nature of us all. Every single person needs to break the chain of sin first.

And then, where is the bird flying? Isaiah 40:31a NIV has the answer. "But those who hope in the Lord will renew their strength. They will soar on wings like eagles."

The direction where a bird will soar must be God, not Abraxas, and the name of God is 'I am who I am.' (Exodus 3:13 NIV)

Abraxas, who leads people to live along with evil, cannot be the name of salvation. Like World Wars, the end of Abraxas is nothing but the ruin of humankind.

There is no salvation in anyone else but Jesus. "God has given no other name under heaven by which we must be saved." (Acts 4:12 NLT)

Memorable Quotes

*Reference Book: Hermann Hesse. (1919). *Demian*. (www.digireads.com: A Digiread.com Book 2013). Kindle E-Book.

(In this e-Book, there are no pages, but Locations are used, therefore, the quotes are noted by L – for location).

- Emil Sinclair's Youth (Preface: L34)
  I wanted only to try to live in obedience to the promptings which came from my true self. Why was that so very difficult?

  The life of everyone is a way to himself, the search for a road, the indication of a path. No man has ever yet attained to self-realisation; yet he strives thereafter, one ploddingly, another with less effort, each as best he can. We can understand one another; but each one is able to explain only himself.

- Chapter 1, L69 (two worlds)
  (the one world)
  This world was for the most part very well known to me; it meant mother and father, love and severity, good example and school. To this world our future had to belong, it had to be crystal-pure, beautiful and well ordered.

(the other world)

In this second world were servant-girls and workmen, ghost stories and breath of scandal. There was a gaily colored flood of monstrous, tempting, terrible, enigmatical goings-on, things such as the slaughter house and prison, drunken men and scolding women, cows in birth-throes, plunging horses, tales of burglaries, murders, suicides.

o Chapter 2, L406 (Cain)
The story of Cain, who carried the mark on his forehead, was it not? Do you like it?

Quite simply! The essential fact, and the point of departure of the story, was the sign.

This man had power, other people shrank from him. He had a 'sign'. One could explain that as one wished. And one always wishes what is convenient and agrees with one's opinions. People were afraid of Cain's children, they had a 'sign.' And so, they explained the sign not as it really was, a distinction, but as the contrary. The fellows with this sign were said to be peculiar, and they were courageous as well.

In short, I mean that Cain was a thundering good fellow, and this story got attached to his name simply because people were afraid of him.

o   Chapter 5, L1386 (Abraxas)
The bird fights its way out of the egg. The egg is the world. Whoever will be born must destroy a world. The bird flies to God. The name of the god is Abraxas.

I sank into deep meditation after I had read the words through several times. It admitted of no doubt: this was Demian's answer.

- Chapter 5, L1416 (the divine and the diabolical)

  "To unite the divine and the diabolical," rang in my ears. Here was a starting-point. I was familiar with that idea from my conversations with Demian in the very last period of our friendship. Demian told me then, we had indeed a God whom we revered, but this God represented part of the world only, the half which was arbitrarily separated from the rest (it was the official, permitted, "bright" world). But one should be able to hold the whole world in honor. One should either have a god who was at the same time a devil, or one should institute devil worship together with worship of God. And now Abraxas was the god, who was at the same time god and devil.

- Chapter 6, L1677 (Pistorius' explanation)

  Sinclair, my dear fellow, the name of our god is Abraxas. He is God and he is Satan; he has the light and the dark world in him.

Abraxas has no objection to urge against any of your ideas or against any of your dreams. Never forget that. But he deserts you if you ever become blameless and normal. He deserts you and seeks out another pot in order to cook his ideas therein.

o Chapter 8, L2546 (World War 1)
Deep down, below the surface of human affairs, something was in process of forming. Something which might be a new order of humanity.

Their deepest and most primitive feelings, even their wildest instincts were not actually directed against the enemy, their murderous and bloody work was an expression of their own inner being, of their cleft soul, which wished to rave and kill, to destroy and die, in order to be able to be born anew. A giant bird was fighting its way out of the egg, and the egg was the world, and the world had to go to ruin.

- o Thomas Mann's comment on *Demian*.

  German novelist Thomas Mann was one of the first intellectuals who realised that Demian "touched so many raw nerves at that time with an uncanny sense of precision, and thus moved an entire young generation with grateful delight, who believed, however wrongly, that this severely insightful author must be a messiah from their midst."

  Retrieved from https://www.dw.com/en/hermann-hesse-demian/a-45775397

Chapter 4 -
The Great Gatsby

Overview

Gatsby's funeral scene sums up the message of this novel. It's reminiscent of Ecclesiastes 1:2 NIV.

> "Meaningless! Meaningless!
> Utterly meaningless'
> Everything is meaningless."

What kind of death do you wish, and how should you live for it?

This book was published in 1925 by F. Scott Fitzgerald, an American novelist. Gatsby, the protagonist, was born into a poor family. When he served as a military officer to get out of poverty, he met Daisy at a party and fell in love with her. His affection conceived tragedy from the beginning because of the difference in social status between the two.

As Gatsby went to war, he lost touch with Daisy. In the meantime, she got married to Tom. He was wealthy and cheated on Daisy. However, she pretended not to be aware of his affair because she didn't want to lose an abundant life.

Gatsby made an enormous fortune by smuggling alcohol during Prohibition after returning from the war. He bought West Egg's mansion close to East Egg, where Daisy lived.

Every weekend, a big party was thrown at Gatsby's place. Gatsby expected Daisy, a party buff, to come to his party one day. Nick was Gatsby's neighbour and becoming a closer friend to him. Gatsby let Nick in on his hidden past, including his love for Daisy.

Gatsby was convinced that Daisy did not love Tom, and he hoped she would come back to him after getting a divorce from her husband. Gatsby would do anything to win Daisy's heart, but Nick could hardly support his blind love for his ex-lover.

One night, the car that Gatsby and Daisy were riding in hit a woman and killed her. She was Tom's mistress called Myrtle. Daisy was driving Gatsby's car, but he concealed who the driver was. Later, Tom visited the late Myrtle's husband, Wilson, and deceived him that Gatsby was the hit-and-run driver.

Furious, Wilson went to Gatsby and shot him dead. Gatsby was killed to protect Daisy, but she went on a trip with Tom without knowing what had happened to her lover. Gatsby had hosted parties for many guests every weekend, but his funeral was lonely.

Except for Nick, Gatsby's father, and some servants, the only other mourner was a man with owl-eyed glasses, but Nick didn't know how the man knew about the funeral.

Biblical Lessons

This story was set in the 1920s in America called the Jazz Age. After World War 1, people enjoyed abundance, like the mellow melody of jazz.

There are two types of characters in the plot. Tom and Daisy were born with a "silver spoon in their mouth", symbolising the wealthy nobility of the old European continent.

On the other hand, Gatsby was a symbol of the American dream. His success from rags to riches and passionate love beyond the social status gap, represents the new world of America.

The title of this novel, The Great Gatsby, may refer to his rise in life. Each reader could have their opinion, but for me, it seems to be about Gatsby's love.

Nick, in the latter part, shouted this to him:

"They're a rotten crowd. You're worth the whole damn bunch put together." (P 123) It was the only compliment Nick ever gave Gatsby because he had always disapproved of him.

But the question Christian readers have is how meaningful his love is. Let's find the answer in the Bible.

Colossians 3:2 NLT says, "Think about the things of heaven, not the things of earth."

Both Gatsby's success and love appear to be great, but the essence is the things of earth. It's just an empty desire like dust that will disappear when the wind blows.

Daisy was more interested in wealth than love itself. The author described her in the opening quotation of the book. "Then wear the gold hat, if that will move her."

Even the moment she reunited with Gatsby, she was touched by the pile of Gatsby's shirts in the cabinet and said, "It makes me sad because I've never seen such—such beautiful shirts before."

Gatsby devoted everything to Daisy but ironically lost not only Daisy but also his life. I believe that the author put a crucial message in Gatsby's funeral, and it's as if he wrote the whole story to show the last funeral scene.

The novel ends with Nick's monologue. "Tomorrow, we will run faster, stretch out our arms farther... So we beat on, boats against the current, borne back ceaselessly into the past."

It will be great if we run faster tomorrow. But if that's all we do, we can't avoid Gatsby's meaningless death either. Readers get an urgent warning about such a vain life.

When we come to Gatsby's funeral scene, we see how futile a life is that is lived for oneself, or only for material gain or human love. It is meaningless, as is lamented in Ecclesiastes 1:2, mentioned at the start of this chapter:

"Meaningless! Meaningless! Utterly meaningless! Everything is meaningless."

Let's examine the first question in the Westminster Shorter Catechism.

"What is the chief end of man?"

Gatsby's story didn't contain the solution, so his life ended in futility. The answer that he had to find was this: "The chief end of man is to glorify God and enjoy Him forever."

Memorable Quotes

*Reference Book:.F. Scott Fitzgerald. (1925). *The Great Gatsby*. (Cabin John: Wildside Press LLC 2021). Kindle E-Book.

- Opening Quotation (P8)
  Then wear the gold hat, if that will move her; If you can bounce high, bounce for her too, till she cry, "Lover, gold-hatted, high-bouncing lover, I must have you!" —THOMAS PARKE D'INVIL-LIERS (the pen name of Fitzgerald)

- Chapter 1, P10 (romantic readiness)
  Only Gatsby, the man who gives his name to this book, was exempt from my reaction—Gatsby who

represented everything for which I have an unaffected scorn.

It was an extraordinary gift for hope, a romantic readiness such as I have never found in any other person and which it is not likely I shall ever find again.

o   Chapter 1, P12 (Gatsby's mansion)
The one on my right was a colossal affair by any standard—it was a factual imitation of some Hôtel de Ville in Normandy, with a tower on one side, spanking new under a thin beard of raw ivy, and a marble swimming pool and more than forty acres of lawn and garden. It was Gatsby's mansion.

o   Chapter 5, P76 (beautiful shirts)
Suddenly with a strained sound, Daisy bent her head into the shirts and began to cry stormily.

"They're such beautiful shirts," she sobbed, her voice muffled in the thick folds. "It makes me sad because I've never seen such—such beautiful shirts before."

- Chapter 8, P122 (I don't think she ever loved him)
  "I don't think she ever loved him." Gatsby turned around from a window and looked at me challengingly. "You must remember, old sport, she was very excited this afternoon. He told her those things in a way that frightened her—that made it look as if I was some kind of cheap sharper. And the result was she hardly knew what she was saying."

  He sat down gloomily. "Of course, she might have loved him, just for a minute, when they were first married—and loved me more even then, do you see?"

- Chapter 8, P123 (You're worth the whole damn bunch)
  We shook hands and I started away. Just before I reached the hedge, I remembered something and turned around.
  "They're a rotten crowd," I shouted across the lawn. "You're worth the whole damn bunch put together."
  I've always been glad I said that. It was the only compliment I ever gave him, because I disapproved of him from beginning to end.

o   Chapter 9, P143 (ending)
Gatsby believed in the green light, the orgastic future that year by year recedes before us. It eluded
us then, but that's no matter—tomorrow we will
run faster, stretch out our arms farther.… And one
fine morning—So we beat on, boats against the
current, borne back ceaselessly into the past.

Chapter 5 -
The Little Prince

Overview

Who is the most precious person to you? *The Little Prince* gives the answer based on both the elderly's wisdom and the children's innocence.

This story was published in 1943 by Antoine de Saint-Exupéry, a French writer and aviator.

The narrator was a pilot, and his plane crash-landed in the desert of Sahara. He came across a little prince there and got to know him.

The little prince came from quite a tiny asteroid known as B-612, where he lived alone. One day, a seed was blown to his planet, and a rose came up. The proud flower tormented him with her vanity. He couldn't stand it any longer, and he left B-612. He stopped by six neighbouring asteroids before finally reaching Earth.

The little prince stumbled on a fox in the desert. The fox said, "If you tame me, then we shall need each other. To me, you will be unique in all the world. To you, I shall be unique in all the world."

Not long before, the little prince had visited a garden that was full of roses. There were as many as five thousand roses in a single place. The little prince went back to them. "You are not at all like my rose. As yet, you are nothing. No one has tamed you, and you have tamed no one."

The little prince learned one secret from the fox. "It is only with the heart that one can see rightly; what is essential is invisible to the eye."

The secret was what the narrator had already experienced in his childhood. When he was six years old, he drew a picture of a boa constrictor digesting an elephant that it swallowed. He showed this painting to the grown-ups and asked whether or not the drawing frightened them. But they answered, "Frighten? Why should anyone be frightened by a hat?"

The inner beauty can only be seen with the heart. At last, the little prince could find the true inner beauty of his rose and decided to return to her. He asked a yellow snake to bite him and thereby kill him with its poisoned teeth. He thought it was the only way he could go back to his asteroid to see his precious rose.

Biblical Lessons

In this story, precious Biblical messages are hidden like treasures. At first, the little prince lived alone on his planet, and the other six asteroids he visited were similar:

A king who always bossed everyone around,
An arrogant person who was eager to blow his own trumpet,
A tippler who drank because he was ashamed of drinking,
A businessman who wanted to own more,
A hectic lamplighter who had to turn a streetlight on and off once a minute,
A geographer who observed from the side.

They could be any one of us. There are billions of people on Earth, but you will live alone if you don't open your heart to neighbours.

The same goes for the church. There are also many lonely and separated people in the Christian community. Some people are no different from the little prince's rose, full of arrogance, vanity and grumbling.

Nevertheless, there is hope in the church. What makes the desert beautiful is that somewhere it hides a well, and the hidden well of the church is Jesus, of course.

In this fiction, the fox plays an important role. He said to the little prince, "I cannot play with you. I am not tamed." "What does that mean, tame?" the little prince asked. "It means to establish ties."

When hearing the fox's answer, the little prince remembered the flower he had left behind. It was the moment the little prince got a new perspective on her.

She was picky, demanding to put her under a glass globe at night and wanting a screen to protect her from the drafts; notwithstanding, she was precious to him because she established ties to him.

Each Christian is like the rose of Jesus, and he is listening to His disciples when they grumble, boast, or sometimes say nothing. There was the relationship of 'tame' between Jesus and the disciples.

'Tame' is related to 'Meek'. Jesus says in Matthew 11:29 KJV, "For I am meek and lowly in heart." The classical Greek word used to translate 'meekness' was to 'tame' horses. (Wikipedia, keyword: meekness)

Therefore, the term 'tame' in this novel serves as a bridge to guide readers to Jesus, meek and lowly in heart.

The little prince was shocked at many roses of the same kind as his flower, but he shouted at them.

"But in herself alone, she is more important than all the hundreds of you other roses.

"You are beautiful, but you are empty. One could not die for you."

His declaration is reminiscent of Jesus' Cross. Anyone without having ties to Jesus is empty. Jesus died for all who would believe in Him. And each and every Christian is a unique and precious rose tamed by Jesus.

Memorable Quotes

*Reference Book: Antoine de Saint-Exupéry. (1943). *The Little Prince*. (Sicily island: GAEditori, 2019). Kindle E-Book.

o   Chapter 1, Page1 (my masterpiece)
I showed my masterpiece to the grown-ups and asked them whether the drawing frightened them. But they answered: "Frighten? Why should anyone be frightened by a hat?" My drawing was not a picture of a hat. It was a picture of a boa constrictor digesting an elephant.

o   Chapter 9, P13 (proud flower)
Then she added: "Don't linger like this. You have decided to go away. Now go!" For she did not want him to see her crying. She was such a proud flower.

o   Chapter 21, P27-28 (tame)
"What does that mean, 'tame'?"
"It is an act too often neglected," said the fox. "It means to establish ties."
"To establish ties?"
"Just that," said the fox. "To me, you are still nothing more than a little boy who is just like a hundred thousand other little boys.

And I have no need of you. And you, on your part, have no need of me. To you, I am nothing more than a fox like a hundred thousand other foxes. But if you tame me, then we shall need each other. To me, you will be unique in all the world. To you, I shall be unique in all the world..."

o Chapter 21, P29 (One could not die for you) The little prince went away, to look again at the roses. "You are not at all like my rose," he said. "As yet you are nothing. No one has tamed you, and you have tamed no one. You are like my fox when I first knew him. He was only a fox like a hundred thousand other foxes. But I have made him my friend, and now he is unique in all the world." And the roses were very much embarrassed. "You are beautiful, but you are empty," he went on. "One could not die for you."

- o Chapter 21, P29 (secret)

  "Goodbye," said the fox. "And now here is my secret, a very simple secret: It is only with the heart that one can see rightly; what is essential is invisible to the eye."

- o Chapter 24, P31 (hiding a well)

  "The desert is beautiful," the little prince added. And that was true. I have always loved the desert. One sits down on a desert sand dune, sees nothing, hears nothing. Yet through the silence something throbs, and gleams...

  "What makes the desert beautiful," said the little prince, "is that somewhere it hides a well..."

Chapter 6 -
The Scarlet Letter

Overview

In John 8, Jesus forgave a woman caught in the act of adultery, allowing her to live a new life. What is your way of dealing with sinners? Is it a scalpel or a sword?

The Scarlet Letter was published in 1850 by Nathaniel Hawthorne, an American novelist. This story was set in Boston, America, in the 17th century. Hester Prynne committed adultery with pastor Dimmesdale and had a baby girl. She never revealed who the father was.

Hester's punishment was harsh, under the influence of Puritanism back then. She was sentenced to have the scarlet letter A for adultery embroidered upon her bosom all her life.

From then on, she devoted herself to helping neighbours in need, while caring for her daughter, Pearl. As time went on, people began to interpret the scarlet A as able.

On the other hand, Dimmesdale suffered from guilt for not revealing that he was Hester's hidden partner.

He was weakened in body and soul, but ironically, the more so, the more touching his sermons were.

Hester had gotten married to Roger Chillingworth in Europe, an old medical scholar. After Hester moved to Boston, he lost contact for two years. Chillingworth belatedly arrived in Boston and found his wife was charged with adultery. When he knew that her partner was Dimmesdale, he wanted to get revenge on the pastor.

Chillingworth played a doctor's role in the village. Later he moved into the pastor's place, pretending to look after him. He hid the fact that he was Hester's husband, and Hester couldn't help but tell Dimmesdale that the doctor was her husband.

The two lovers planned to flee to Europe, but Dimmesdale changed his mind to atone for his sin publicly. After the inauguration service of the governor of New England, the minister confessed his sin in the marketplace. The novel suggested that the letter A was mysteriously stigmatised on his bare chest. He was dying in Hester's arms. Chillingworth also passed away not long after losing the subject of revenge.

Hester and her daughter moved over to England, and Hester alone came back to Boston later. As many years passed, Hester passed away and a new grave was formed near the old and sunken grave of Dimmesdale. One tombstone served for both;

ON A FIELD, SABLE,

THE LETTER A, GULES.

(Sable is darkbrown, symbolising the sin of Dimmesdale. Gules is heraldic red, the red of Hester's Adultery.)

Biblical Lessons

Suppose you have a sword and scalpel in your hand. What would you like to use to deal with sinners? Both are the same in that they hate sin. But a scalpel aims to restore sinners, while a sword intends to kill them.

The Boston Puritans tried to destroy Hester's whole life by stigmatising the Scarlet Letter A in this story. They had swords in their hands.

First of all, let's make one point clear. The Puritans are fundamentally exemplary and admirable, and they pursue Biblical values in their daily lives.

When Puritanism works appropriately, it can be a driving force to achieve a holy life. But if strict religious disciplines come first, God's grace is gone.

Jesus taught the valuable lesson in John chapter 8.

There was a woman caught in the act of adultery, and people asked Jesus if they would stone her according to the law of Moses.

Jesus said, "All right, but let the one who has never sinned throw the first stone." (John 8:7 NLT)

When the accusers heard this, they slipped away one by one. Then Jesus said to the woman, "Didn't even one of them condemn you? Neither do I. Go and sin no more."

Don't get Him wrong! In this case, Jesus did not tolerate the sin itself. He drew a line, saying, "Go and sin no more."

Nevertheless, Jesus put priority on her salvation, and his forgiveness would not only allow her to start anew but also prevent her from committing any more sins.

As Hester's life changed, the meaning of the Scarlet Letter A turned to 'able', not adultery. She accepted all the disgrace and humiliation and continued to stay in the community rather than fleeing.

Although she was poor, she helped others in need. When pestilence stalked through the town, there were none as devoted as Hester. The world's heavy hand ordained her as a Sister of Mercy.

Unlike Hester, the pastor Dimmesdale, who hid his sin, had to live a hellish life for seven years until his death. He would have experienced heavenly peace at the very moment he confessed his sin.

Act 2:38 NLT says, "Each of you must repent of your sins and turn to God, and be baptised in the name of Jesus Christ for the forgiveness of your sins."

God has already forgiven you even before you repent of your sins. But you can only enjoy the grace of forgiveness once you repent – turn your back on sin.

Isaiah 1:18 NLT says, "Though your sins are like scarlet, I will make them as white as snow. Though they are red like crimson, I will make them as white as wool."

The 17th-century Bostonians in *The Scarlet Letter* overlooked God's grace to turn scarlet sin into white wool or snow. What about you in the 21st century? Is there a sword or scalpel in your hand?

Memorable Quotes

*Reference Book: Nathaniel Hawthorne. (1850). *The Scarlet Letter*. (Seattle: Amazon Classics). Kindle E-Book

- Chapter 2, P53 (scarlet letter A)
  Lastly, in lieu of these shifting scenes, came back the rude marketplace of the Puritan settlement, with all the towns-people assembled and levelling their stern regards at Hester Prynne, —yes, at herself, —who stood on the scaffold of the pillory, an infant on her arm, and the letter A, in scarlet, fantastically embroidered with gold-thread, upon her bosom!

- Chapter 13, P146 (A for Able)
  The letter was the symbol of her calling. Such helpfulness was found in her, —so

much power to do, and power to sympathise, —that many people refused to interpret the scarlet A by its original signification. They said that it meant Able; so strong was Hester Prynne, with a woman's strength.

o Chapter 17, P173 (nothing but despair)
After a while, the minister fixed his eyes on Hester Prynne's. "Hester," said he, "hast thou found peace?" She smiled drearily, looking down upon her bosom. "Hast thou?" she asked. "None! —nothing but despair!" he answered.

o Chapter 17, P174 (penance or penitence)
"No, Hester, no!" replied the clergyman. "There is no substance in it! It is cold and dead, and can do nothing for me! of penance, I have had enough! of penitence, there has been none! Else, I should long ago have thrown off these garments of mock holiness, and have shown myself to mankind as they will see me at the judgment-seat.

o Chapter 23, P229 (confession)

"People of New England!" cried he, with a voice that rose over them, high, solemn, and majestic, —yet had always a tremor through it, and sometimes a shriek, struggling up out of a fathomless depth of remorse and woe, —"ye, that have loved me! —ye, that have deemed me holy! —behold me here, the one sinner.

o Chapter 23, P230 (It was revealed!)

With a convulsive motion, he tore away the ministerial band from before his breast. It was revealed! But it was irreverent to describe that revelation. For an instant, the gaze of the horror-stricken multitude was concentred on the ghastly miracle; while the minister stood, with a flush of triumph in his face, as one who, in the crisis of acutest pain, had won a victory.

o Chapter 24, P237 (one tombstone for two graves)

Yet one tombstone served for both. All around, there were monuments carved with armorial bearings; and on this simple slab of slate—as the curious investigator may still discern, and perplex himself with the purport—there appeared the semblance of an engraved escutcheon. It bore a device, a herald's wording of which might serve for a motto and brief description of our now concluded legend; so sombre is it, and relieved only by one ever-glowing point of light gloomier than the shadow: —
ON A FIELD, SABLE, THE LETTER A, GULES.

Chapter 7 -
Uncle Tom's Cabin

Overview

This tragic story exposes the miserable lives of African American slaves in the mid-19th century. Tom, the main character, was thrust into inhumane slavery. How did he live his life as a Christian slave?

Uncle Tom's Cabin was published in 1852 by Harriet Beecher Stowe, an American novelist. Let's review the story.

A Kentucky farmer named Arthur Shelby ran up massive debts, so he had to sell two of his slaves, Tom and the young son of his wife's servant Eliza, to a slave trader. Tom accepted his fate of being sold, but Eliza ran away with her son that night.

While Tom was aboard a boat on the way to auction in New Orleans, he saved the life of a little girl named Eva, who fell off the ship.

Her grateful father bought Tom from the slave merchant. Eva was a true-hearted Christian who couldn't be kinder to Tom. Eva's health, constantly frail, rapidly began to decline. On her deathbed, she asked her father to set Tom free.

Her dad made plans to do so, but he was stabbed to death before taking the step for Tom's freedom. Eva's mother sold Tom to Simon Legree, the worst master who brutally treated his slaves.

Legree tried to use Tom as a supervisor because he had a good reputation among slaves. The evil master commanded Tom to whip one of the slaves, but he refused. So, he was beaten instead.

Two female slaves, Cassy and Emmeline, could no longer stand Legree's sexual exploitation and fled the plantation.

Legree flogged Tom severely to find the whereabouts of the runaway slaves. Eventually, Tom was whipped to his death, keeping the secret to the end.

The first master's son, George Shelby, visited Legree to repurchase Tom, but Tom died in front of him. After returning to his Kentucky farm, George set all of his slaves free.

Biblical Lessons

In this story, Tom was a faithful Christian who always read the Bible and lived the Biblical life under any circumstances.

He even forgave his cruel master, Legree, after he was fatally beaten. He said, dying, "Oh, if he only could repent, the Lord would forgive him now; but I'm feared he never will!" (P249)

It was reminiscent of Jesus' forgiveness on the Cross. "Father, forgive them, for they don't know what they are doing." (Luke 23:34 NLT)

Stephen's prayer also comes to mind. He prayed for forgiveness while being stoned to death. "Lord, don't charge them with this sin!" (Acts 7:60 NLT).

Forgiveness *was* also found at the scene of the Holocaust.

There was a Jewish concentration camp under Nazi Germany, located in the village of Ravensbrück from 1939 to 1945. It was exclusively for women. (Ref: Wikipedia, keyword: Ravensbrück concentration camp)

One day, a scrap of paper was found in the clothing of the dead body of a Jewish girl in the camp.

(https://thomasandbede.com/a-prayer-from-a-
jewish-victim-at-ravensbruck/)

"O Lord, remember, not only the men and
women of good will but also those of ill will.
But do not remember all the suffering
they have inflicted on us;
remember the fruits we have borne,
thanks to this suffering:
our comradeship, our loyalty,
our humility, our courage, our generosity,
the greatness of heart
which has grown out of all this,
and when they come to judgement,
let all the fruits we have borne
be their forgiveness."

Some activists criticise that Tom's way of life,
which ended in a tragic death, never helps improve
human rights.

From their point of view, Tom's story may be nothing more than a sermon that can be heard in the
church.

But what can change history eventually?

In November 1862, during the Civil War (April 12, 1861 – May 9, 1865), President Lincoln called Mrs Stowe, the author, to Washington and said,

"So, you're the little woman who wrote the book that started this great war."

Jesus' Cross may look weak, but it has the strongest power to defeat evil forces. Wouldn't it be clear that Jesus' way can change history if *Uncle Tom's Cabin* served as an opportunity to break down the stronghold of slavery?

Memorable Quotes

*Reference Book: Harriet Beecher Stowe. (1852). *Uncle Tom's Cabin*. (A Public Domain Book / Downloaded from Kindle E-Book.)

- o Chapter 1, P3 (Tom)
  No; I mean, really, Tom is a good, steady, sensible, pious fellow. He got religion at a camp-meeting, four years ago; and I believe he really did get it. I've trusted him, since then, with everything I have —money,

house, horses— and let him come and go round the country; and I always found him true and square in everything.

o   Chapter 7, P33 (praying for a slave dealer)
And Aunt Chloe covered her face with her checked apron, and began to sob in good earnest. "Pray for them that 'spitefully use you, the good book says," says Tom.

o   Chapter 33, P212 (My soul an't yours)
Mas'r, if you mean to kill me, kill me; but, as to my raising my hand agin anyone here, I never shall, —I'll die first!"
"An't yer mine, now, body and soul?" he said, giving Tom a violent kick with his heavy boot; "tell me!"
"No! no! no! my soul an't yours, Mas'r! You haven't bought it, —ye can't buy it! It's been bought and paid for, by one that is able to keep it; —no matter, no matter, you can't harm me!"

o Chapter 41, P249 (the Lord would forgive him)

"O, don't! —oh, ye mustn't!" said Tom, grasping his hand; "he's a poor mis'able critter! It's awful to think on't! Oh, if he only could repent, the Lord would forgive him now; but I'm 'feared he never will!"

"Who, —who, —who shall separate us from the love of Christ?" he said, in a voice that contended with mortal weakness; and, with a smile, he fell asleep.

o Chapter 44, P260 (Be Christian as he was) Think of your freedom, every time you see UNCLE TOM'S CABIN; and let it be a memorial to put you all in mind to follow in his steps, and be honest and faithful and Christian as he was.

Chapter 8 -
The Secret Garden

Overview

Nobody liked the little girl called Mary, but when the secret garden was opened, she dramatically changed into a lovely girl and even saved a miserable boy's fading life. Is there a secret garden in your heart? Why don't you open it up? You will be able to start a new life.

This book was published in 1911 by Frances Hodgson Burnett, a British novelist. Let's get into the secret garden together.

Mary Lenox was a 10-year-old British girl who grew up in India. Her mother was a party buff and only cared about entertaining herself. All the servants let the girl do whatever she wanted, so Mary became a spoiled, rude and bad-tempered child.

The cholera epidemic broke out in India. Her parents and most of the servants died, and the servants that survived ran away. Now there was no one left to look after her in India.

Mary was sent to her uncle, Mr Craven, at Misselthwaite Manor, Yorkshire, England. He travelled abroad most of the time, so she hardly saw him.

The Manor was full of darkness, and it had been a long time since the vitality of life disappeared. Mary heard a cry in the wind at night.

At the Manor, there was a secret garden that had been closed for the past decade. It used to be Mrs Craven's Garden. She was sitting on the branch of a tree when it broke, and she fell. She was seriously injured and died. Since then, Mr Craven closed it for good and forbade anyone to mention it.

Mary came across the key to the secret garden door and finally entered the garden! She met with Dickon, who loved nature and even communicated with animals. Together, they recultivated the secret garden.

One night, she heard the cry again. She searched for it and found a boy crying, who was Colin, Mr Craven's son. Colin was always sick and stayed in bed, and he was afraid he would grow up to be a hunchback and die not long afterwards.

But, after Mary and Dickon took Colin into the secret garden, his life changed. He felt his fear leave him and remained standing on the ground. When Mr Craven returned home, the secret garden door burst open, and Colin ran out. His son led his father into the garden and told him how the magic made him strong and well.

Colin walked with his dad as firmly and steadily as any boy in Yorkshire.

Biblical Lessons

It's a novel that makes you smile as you turn the last page. As the secret garden opened, the gloomy mood of the narrative changed to a revitalising tone.

This fantastic twist is reminiscent of chapter 47 of Ezekiel. The water flowing out of the temple rose to the ankles, knees, and waist to become a deep river. Everywhere the water reached, all things came back to life.

Therefore, when you see someone trapped in the dark, you have a word to say. "Open up your secret garden first."

The first person that experienced the revival was Mary. When selfish thorns were removed from her mind, she could have enough space in her heart for someone else.

The same thing happened to Colin. When he got out of the room and entered the secret garden, he changed into a completely different boy.

"That night Colin slept without once awakening, and when he opened his eyes in the morning, he lay still and smiled without knowing it—smiled because he felt so curiously comfortable." (Chapter 19, P156)

Colin's soul, which was fading in bed, was resurrected. When he joined working in the garden, the light drove darkness out of his life, and he called it the magic of the secret garden.

He cried out, "I shall get well! I shall get well! Mary! Dickon! I shall get well! And I shall live forever and ever and ever!" (Chapter 20, P169)

When the secret garden opened, everything began to come to life. Colin's revival moved on to his father. When Mr Craven talked with his son, the father laughed until tears came into his eyes and sometimes tears came into his eyes when he was not laughing.

Their broken relationship has recovered. Here's the last scene.

"Across the lawn came the Master of Misselthwaite, and he looked as many of them had never seen him. And by his side with his head up in the air and his eyes full of laughter walked as strongly and steadily as any boy in Yorkshire—Master Colin." (Chapter 27, P234)

The opening of the secret garden suggests the light that opened the prelude to creation.

Read Genesis 1:2,3 NLT: "The earth was formless and empty, and darkness covered the deep waters. And the Spirit of God was hovering over the surface of the waters. Then God said, 'Let there be light,' and there was light."

Martha and Dickon, who helped Mary, were poor but happy. Happiness doesn't rely on money, and it's up to whether or not you open up yourself to your neighbours.

In this competitive world, people try to beat others for their success. Even if they live in the same space, they are only competitors to each other. This way of life will eventually destroy them.

Proverbs 14:12 NLT says, "There is a path before each person that seems right, but it ends in death." If you have a secret garden in your life, open the door immediately! That's the way to lead you to life.

Memorable Quotes

*Reference Book: Frances Hodgson Burnett. (1911). *The Secret Garden.* (Seattle: Amazon Classics. design by Jeff Miller, Faceout Studio). Kindle E-Book.

- o Chapter 1, P5 (disagreeable-looking child)
  When Mary Lennox was sent to Misselthwaite Manor to live with her uncle, everybody said she was the most disagreeable-looking child ever seen.

- o Chapter 2, P16 (crooked back)
  She stopped herself as if she had just remembered something in time. "He's got a crooked back," she said. "That set him wrong. He was

a sour young man and got no good of all his money and big place till he was married."

o Chapter 12, P93 (not so much a hunchback)
She could see that the man in the chair was not so much a hunchback as a man with high, rather crooked shoulders, and he had black hair streaked with white.

o Chapter 8, P83 (secret garden)
No one was coming. No one ever did come, it seemed, and she took another long breath because she could not help it, and she held back the swinging curtain of ivy and pushed back the door which opened slowly—slowly. Then she slipped through it, and shut it behind her, and stood with her back against it, looking about her and breathing quite fast with excitement, and wonder, and delight. She was standing inside the secret garden.

o   Chapter 19, P156 (Colin)

That night Colin slept without once awakening, and when he opened his eyes in the morning, he lay still and smiled without knowing it— smiled because he felt so curiously comfortable.

o   Chapter 20, P168 (I shall get well!)

"I shall get well! I shall get well!" he cried out. "Mary! Dickon! I shall get well! And I shall live forever and ever and ever!"

o   Chapter 22, P180 (Am I a hunchback?)

"Look at me!" he commanded. "Look at me all over! Am I a hunchback? Have I got crooked legs?" Ben Weatherstaff had not quite got over his emotion, but he had recovered a little and answered almost in his usual way. "Not tha'," he said. "Everyone thought I was going to die," said Colin shortly. "I'm not!"

- Chapter 27, P234 (ending)

Across the lawn came the Master of Misselthwaite, and he looked as many of them had never seen him. And by his side with his head up in the air and his eyes full of laughter walked as strongly and steadily as any boy in Yorkshire—Master Colin.

Chapter 9 -
Crime and Punishment

Overview

Crime And Punishment was published in 1866 by Fyodor Dostoevsky, a Russian novelist known to be an Orthodox Christian. Let's find out what crime happened first.

Raskolnikov, the main character, thought that he was an extraordinary person like Napoleon. He didn't associate with others, being isolated from society.

He dropped out of college because of poverty. He pawned his father's silver watch and a gold ring, a present from his sister. Alyona, a pawnbroker, paid him very little, and Raskolnikov hated such exploitation.

Alyona was nothing but a harmful louse to him, and he thought she deserved to be punished and finally killed her.

But something unexpected happened. Lizaveta, the pawnbroker's sister, accidentally witnessed the murder, so he had no choice but to kill her, too. He became obsessed with guilt that he had killed an innocent person.

Porfiry, the head of the Investigation, suspected Raskolnikov of the murderer. When Porfiry interrogated him, Raskolnikov defended himself with intelligence and avoided being charged. However, his guilt grew more over time.

Raskolnikov had a fateful meeting with Sonia, daughter of alcoholic Marmeladov. She had to work as a prostitute because she was the only breadwinner in the family.

When Raskolnikov confessed to his crime, Sonia urged him to stand on the crossroads and say to everyone, "I am a murderer!"

Eventually, Raskolnikov turned himself in to the police. He was sent away to Siberia for a term of eight years in prison with hard labour. Sonia followed him all the way and looked after him.

Raskolnikov realised that he truly loved her. The pair waited for the remaining years of his prison term.

One day, Raskolnikov read the New Testament that Sonya, a faithful Christian, had given him, and which he kept beneath his pillow. That's when he began a new life.

Biblical Lessons

The lesson of this story can be understood more clearly when comparing to the Scripture that Satan tempted Jesus in Luke 4.

Firstly, what comes first?

The devil tempted Jesus, who fasted for forty days. "If you are the Son of God, tell this stone to become a loaf of bread." (Luke 4:3 NLT) Jesus declined the temptation firmly. "People do not live by bread alone."

What would Raskolnikov have done if he was in the same situation? He was as poor as a church mouse and despised the pawnbroker Alyona to the point of killing her.

If Satan had urged Raskolnikov to make bread out of stone, he would've done so if he could.

However, Jesus clarified what should come first. When God sits on the throne of our lives, He will surely take care of our bread issues.

Matthew 6:33 NIV says, "But seek first his kingdom and his righteousness, and all these things will be given to you as well."

Secondly, who do you worship?

The devil showed Jesus all the kingdoms of the world and said he would give Jesus them all if Jesus worshipped him. (Luke 4:5-7)

It was not Satan's bluff. When Adam ate the Forbidden fruit, his kingship over the world was handed over to Satan. (Luke 4:6, John 12:31) Jesus, in Luke 4:8 NIV, proclaimed, "Worship the Lord your God and serve him only."

Let's think about Raskolnikov. He wanted to prove his superiority by killing the old pawnbroker. For him, Napoleon's splendour was an object of admiration, and Raskolnikov would worship anything if it made him a superhuman being.

Lastly, what motivates you?

Satan took Jesus to Jerusalem, to the highest point of the temple and demanded to jump off. Satan claimed that Jesus should be all right if He is the Son of God. (Luke 4:9-11)

Jesus refused. "You must not test the Lord your God." (Luke 4:12 NLT). Jesus overcame all the temptations.

It was a shame that Raskolnikov didn't. His ulterior motive for the murder was to become a Napoleon by killing her.

He was convinced that he would never get caught because he planned a perfect crime with superior intelligence.

But what happened? He couldn't avoid Porfiry's suspicion, and unexpected guilt captured him. Above all, Sonia's unfailing love melted his frozen heart. Raskolnikov's criminal plan, which he was proud of being perfect, was all messed up.

Jesus didn't attempt to prove that He is the Son of God. He didn't have to do that because He is "I AM Who I AM." (Exodus 3:14 NIV)

In contrast, Raskolnikov tried to show off his intelligence to prove his superiority, and the arrogance led him to commit murder.

If God's grace had not come to him in the clothes of Sonia's love, his life would have been ruined.

Crime And Punishment, the title of this novel, is not enough to cover the entire story. The ultimate title should be *Crime, Punishment and Grace*, I believe.

Memorable Quotes

*Reference Book: Fyodor Dostoevsky. (1866). *Crime And Punishment*. (First digital edition 2018 by Gianluca Ruffini). Kindle E-Book.

- Part 1, Chapter 4, P31 (Raskolnikov)
  He was very poor, and there was a sort of haughty pride and reserve about him, as though he were keeping something to himself. He seemed to some of his comrades to look down upon them all as children, as though he were superior in development, knowledge and convictions, as though their beliefs and interests were beneath him.

- Part 1, Chapter 6, P40 (Alyona)
  Besides, what value has the life of that sickly, stupid, ill-natured old woman in the balance of existence! No more than the life of a louse, of

a black-beetle, less in fact because the old woman is doing harm. She is wearing out the lives of others; the other day she bit Lizaveta's finger out of spite; it almost had to be amputated.

o Part 5, Chapter 4, P235 (I wanted to become a Napoleon)
He looked at her with anguish. "What if it were really that?" he said, as though reaching a conclusion. "Yes, that's what it was! I wanted to become a Napoleon, that is why I killed her.... Do you understand now?"

o Part 6, Chapter 8, P297 (He knelt)
He knelt down in the middle of the square, bowed down to the earth, and kissed that filthy earth with bliss and rapture. He got up and bowed down a second time.

- Part 6, Chapter 8, P300 (Raskolnikov turned himself in)

  It was I killed the old pawnbroker woman and her sister Lizaveta with an axe and robbed them." Ilya Petrovitch opened his mouth. People ran up on all sides. Raskolnikov repeated his statement.

- Epilogue, P309 (New Testament)

  Under his pillow lay the New Testament. He took it up mechanically. The book belonged to Sonia; it was the one from which she had read the raising of Lazarus to him.

  But that is the beginning of a new story, the story of the gradual renewal of a man, the story of his gradual regeneration, of his passing from one world into another, of his initiation into a new unknown life. That might be the subject of a new story, but our present story is ended.

Part B

Short Stories

Chapter 10 - Ivan the Fool

Overview

Judging by secular values, the path of Jesus looks foolish. Jesus' followers could also be regarded as fools from a worldly perspective. Are you willing to live a silly way of life, too?

Ivan The Fool was written in 1886 by Lev Nikolayevich Tolstoy, a Russian writer known to be a Christian anarchist. Let's look into Ivan's story to find the answer to how to live.

There was a rich peasant with three sons and a daughter. The eldest Simeon was a soldier, and the second was a merchant named Tarras. Ivan, the youngest son, was a fool and took care of the home as a farmer. His daughter Milania was born mute.

The old devil was unhappy that Ivan's brothers were living in peace. He summoned three little devils to break up Ivan's family, and they went into action.

The first imp gave Simeon the reckless ambition to conquer the world with military force. Simeon's pipe dream was supposed to fail, and he went to jail after all.

The second imp made Tarras greedy enough to purchase whatever he wished. Finally, he was left with an enormous debt.

However, Ivan welcomed the two who came to ask for help, and the family could maintain a peaceful relationship. Ivan was a pain in the neck for the devils.

The third imp took over the baton. The devil tried to stop Ivan from working by causing a severe stomach ache. But it was useless because the fool continued to work despite the pain.

When the little demon was caught red-handed by Ivan, he barely spared his life by giving three roots that could cure any disease.

One day, Ivan heard that the czar's daughter was terminally ill, and he volunteered to treat her, relying on the roots he received from the imp.

However, just before he arrived at the palace, no root was left because he had already used the last one to heal a poor woman. Even so, the princess got well miraculously as soon as he got into the palace. Ivan became the czar's son-in-law and ascended to the throne after the czar died.

Now the old devil himself took action to ruin Ivan's family. He had ruined the two elder brothers and moved on to Ivan. He targeted the only custom of Ivan's kingdom; the men with toil-hardened hands are always the first, while the possessors of soft white hands are the next.

The demon disguised as a gentleman said that working with the head could give a better life than working with hands. Ivan's people didn't understand his point. The old devil became weary, hitting his head against a pole. At last, people said, "The gentleman has commenced to work with his head."

The evil one fell headlong and disappeared, leaving a hole in the ground.

Biblical Lessons

So, Ivan the fool defeated all the demons. Ivan didn't claim his rights for his sake and accepted whatever his brothers demanded. Ivan ascended to the throne, but he was still silly. How on earth would he rule the kingdom? Tolstoy showed that the foolish way would rather be the wisest in the world.

God's kingdom can be understood in the same vein. 1 Corinthians 1:27 NIV says, "But God chose the foolish things of the world to shame the wise." Jesus said, "It is more blessed to give than to receive." (Acts 20:35 NIV)

Let's remember the Christian way is different from the worldly-wise way. Don't be ashamed of living a foolish life. God chose to entrust His mission to those who lived like Ivan as servants.

Many people think living a life of comfort without working would be a blessed life. In this regard, wealthy people or lottery winners are looked upon with envy.

What is the Biblical view about work?

Genesis 2:15 NIV says, "The Lord God took the man and put him in the Garden of Eden to work it and take care of it."

Paul says, "We worked night and day, labouring and toiling so that we would not be a burden to any of you." (2 Thessalonians 3:8 NIV)

In 2 Thessalonians 3:10 NIV, he makes the point more straightforward. "The one who is unwilling to work shall not eat."

God designed human beings to work. Even in the Garden of Eden, a perfect paradise, labour was part of Adam's life. Paul worked not only as a missionary but also as a tentmaker. In this short story, Ivan's life goes along with the Biblical context.

This story, on the face of it, seems to respect physical work more than intellectual work. However, as you read between the lines, you will find that it is not true.

Since manual labour is easily neglected at work, Ivan's story leads readers to value all kinds of toil.

Tolstoy shows the ideal community he dreamed of through Ivan's Kingdom. His idea is connected with the image of heaven.

As is often imagined, Heaven is not a place only to bum around. It's the opposite. The wealthy inhabitants of God's kingdom are hard workers. All children of God will have the honour to participate in God's work. Jesus said, "My Father is always working, and so am I." (John 5:17 NLT)

Memorable Quotes

*Reference Book: Lev Nikolayevich Tolstoy. (1886). *Ivan The Fool.* (www.feedbooks.com: Feedbooks version) Translated by L. and A. Maude. Kindle E-Book.

- o P5 (old devil and three imps)
  It was disappointing to the Stary Tchert (Old Devil) that the brothers did not quarrel over the division of the property, and that they separated peacefully; and he cried out, calling his three small devils (Tchertionki).

- o P8 (healing roots)
  "I am dreadfully sick at my stomach. Can you cure me?" "I can," the little devil said. "Then do so."

  The little devil bent toward the earth and began searching for roots, and when he found them, he gave them to Ivan, saying: "If you will swallow some of these you will be immediately cured of whatsoever disease you are afflicted with."

o P24 (King the Fool)
The people soon learned that Ivan was a fool. His wife one day said to him, "The people say you are a fool, Ivan." "Well, let them think so if they wish," he replied.

His wife pondered this reply for some time, and at last decided that if Ivan was a fool, she also was one, and that it would be useless to go contrary to her husband, thinking affectionately of the old proverb that "where the needle goes there goes the thread also."

o P24 (They lived peacefully together)
Seeing that Ivan was a fool, all the wise men left the kingdom and only the fools remained. They had no money, their wealth consisting only of the products of their labor. But they

lived peacefully together, supported them-
selves in comfort, and had plenty to spare for
the needy and afflicted.

o   P37 (working with his head)
One day, while the old devil was standing on
the balcony, he became weak, and, falling
down, hurt his head against a pole.

Seeing this, one of the fools ran to Ivan's wife
and said, "The gentleman has at last commenced to work with his head." She ran to the
field to tell Ivan, who was much surprised, and
said, "Let us go and see him."

o   P37 (only one custom)
There is only one unchangeable custom observed in Ivan's kingdom: The man with toil-
hardened hands is always given a seat at the ta-
ble, while the possessor of soft white hands
must be contented with what is left.

Chapter 11 - The Black Cat

Overview

It is easy for the fury to explode uncontrollably when evil spirits add fuel to the fire. If such a thing happens, it is too late for you to go back. That horror occurred to the protagonist of *The Black Cat.*

This narrative was written in 1843 by Edgar Allan Poe, an American short-story writer. What follows is a shortened and simplified version of the full story.

This story is my, the protagonist's, confession: From my infancy, I have been gentle and especially fond of animals. I had a big and beautiful cat, entirely black, called Pluto, and he followed me wherever I walked around the house.

One night, I returned home much intoxicated, and the cat gave a slight wound upon my hand with his teeth. The fury of a demon instantly possessed me, and I took a pen-knife from my pocket and gouged out one of its eyes.

The next day, I was stunned to see what I had done. Pluto was avoiding me in extreme terror. As I looked at it, the feeling of guilt soon gave place to irritation; finally, I hung the cat's neck to a tree in the garden.

That night, a fire broke out in my house. I found the figure of a cat with a rope around its neck on the unburned surface of a wall.

Months later, a cat resembling Pluto followed me home from a pub, and it domesticated itself at once.

One day my wife accompanied me into the cellar, and the cat entered under my feet and nearly threw me headlong. It drove me crazy. Uplifting an axe, I aimed a blow at the animal, but by mistake, I buried the axe in my wife's brain.

I deposited her body between the outer and inner walls of the basement. I looked for the cat, but it did not make its appearance anywhere.

A party of the police came to investigate my wife's disappearance. When the police couldn't find anything suspicious in my house, I got excited, satisfied with my perfect crime.

I rapped heavily, with my cane upon that very portion of the brick-work where I hid the corpse of the wife.

Then a bizarre cry echoed through the wall into the cellar. When the police broke down the wall, the body of my wife turned up. And a live cat was sitting on top of it!

Isn't it a scary story? How did a soft-hearted person turn into such a terrifying monster?

Biblical Lessons

The protagonist's behaviour grew more violent. At first, he gouged out one of Pluto's eyes, then hung its neck to a tree, and finally, he killed his wife by putting an axe into her brain, even though it was an unintended crime.

The worst thing is he did not repent after committing murder. He even got excited about his perfect crime when the police couldn't find his wife's body.

What made him such an awful person? Alcohol can be the initial cause, but it is not a decisive one.

The author wrote the hidden reason, saying, "The fury of a demon instantly possessed me. I knew myself no longer. My original soul seemed, at once, to take its flight from my body."

The Bible confirms it clearly through Ephesians 6:12 NIV.

"For our struggle is not against flesh and blood, but against the rulers, against the authorities, against the powers of this dark world and against the spiritual forces of evil in the heavenly realms."

This story deals with an anger issue. In the Bible, the first person with an anger disorder was Cain.

In Genesis chapter 4, Cain and his brother Abel offered sacrifices to God. But when the Lord accepted only Abel's, Cain was angry, and his face was downcast.

God said to him, "If you do not do what is right, sin is crouching at your door; it desires to have you, but you must rule over it." (Genesis 4:7 NIV)

Even so, Cain failed to take control of anger and killed Abel in the field. There must've been an evil spirit behind Cain's uncontrollable anger.

Ephesians 4:31 NLT says, "Get rid of all bitterness, rage, anger, harsh words, and slander, as well as all types of evil behaviour."

People are losing patience and moderation more and more, such as hot-tempered bosses, aggressive customers, abusive parents, crazy drivers, etc.

What does the Bible teach us? First of all, you must confess your sins to the Lord like David did in Psalm 32:5 NLT.

"I said to myself, 'I will confess my rebellion to the Lord.' And you forgave me! All my guilt is gone."

Debris sink down only when the water becomes still. When you feel you are on the verge of getting angry, stop immediately, stay still, and look up at God.

In Psalm 62:1 ESV, David says, "For God alone, my soul waits in silence; from him comes my salvation."

May God's salvation that restored David's soul come down upon all of you!

Memorable Quotes

*Reference Book: Edgar Allan Poe. (1843). *The Black Cat*. Retrieved from

https://poestories.com/read/blackcat

o   cutting one of its eyes

I seized him; when, in his fright at my violence, he gave a slight wound upon my hand with his teeth.

The fury of a demon instantly possessed me. I knew myself no longer. I took from my pocket a pen-knife, opened it, grasped the poor beast by the neck, and deliberately cut one of its eyes from the socket!

o   hanging it to a tree

The next day, I was stunned to see what I had done. Pluto, who had lost one eye, was avoiding me in extreme terror. As I looked at it, the feeling of guilt soon gave place to irritation.

Finally, I slipped a noose about its neck and hung it to a tree in the garden.

o   burying the axe in her brain

It exasperated me to madness. Uplifting an axe, in my wrath, I aimed a blow at the animal. But this blow was arrested by the hand of my wife. Goaded, by the interference, into a rage more than demoniacal, I withdrew my arm from her grasp and buried the axe in her brain.

o   a live cat sitting on top of it
Then a bizarre cry echoed through the wall into the cellar. When the police broke down the wall, the body of his wife turned up. And a live cat was sitting on top of it.

Part C

A Fairy Tale

Chapter 12 -
Aladdin and The Wonderful Lamp

Overview

When you say that you follow Jesus, does it not mean that you want someone to do everything for you, like Aladdin's lamp genie? Read this fairy tale to find the answer to this most critical question in faith.

Aladdin and the Wonderful Lamp is one of the folktales included in One Thousand and One Nights or Arabian Nights.

The story was set in China. There was a poor boy called Aladdin. One day, a magician came to see him, pretending to be his uncle.

The fake uncle asked Aladdin to bring a lamp from the underground cave. The lamp had magic power, and the wizard could only get it through a third party. He put a magic ring on the boy's finger just in case.

Aladdin found the lamp in the cave, but he didn't hand it to the uncle because he had a bad hunch. Sure enough, the magician blocked the cave, flying into a rage.

With the help of the ring genie, Aladdin was able to get out of the cave and return home with the lamp.

When his mother polished the old lamp for sale, a hideous genie appeared. Thanks to the genie, Aladdin learnt of the lamp's secret and enjoyed a wealthy life with his mother.

One day, he ran into a princess passing by on the street and fell in love with her at first sight. For a marriage proposal, Aladdin presented the king with lots of jewels. After twists and turns, the princess finally became his wife.

The sorcerer came back to obtain the magic lamp. He got his hands on the lamp, but Aladdin regained it thanks to the ring genie. Aladdin ascended to the throne after the king died.

Biblical Lessons

How did you experience this story? Do you also want to get the magic lamp? The lamp genie seems almighty but is only a servant to anyone who owns him. It is entirely different from the Christian faith. The turning point lies in the question of who the master is.

Ephesians 6:6 NLT says, "As slaves of Christ, do the will of God with all your heart." 1 Corinthians 7:22 NIV says, "The one who was free when called is Christ's slave."

The Bible proclaims that God is the master; we are His servants. Jesus is not just an omnipotent helper like a lamp genie. As we confess in Romans 10:9 NIV, Jesus is my Lord (Master).

"If you declare with your mouth, 'Jesus is Lord,' and believe in your heart that God raised him from the dead, you will be saved."

The genie fetches whatever Aladdin wishes. This story supports the idea that "The more, the better." Is it the same as the Christian point of view?

What God cares about is not your greed but your need. Read Philippians 4:19 NIV. "And my God will meet all your needs according to the riches of his glory in Christ Jesus."

In Proverbs 30:8 NIV, Agur also shows the same viewpoint. "Give me neither poverty nor riches, but give me only my daily bread."

We still can say, "The more, the better." But we need to remember the lesson of 2 Corinthians 8:15

NLT. "Those who gathered a lot had nothing left over, and those who gathered only a little had enough."

The Lord gives more to some people so that they may give what is left to those in need.

Aladdin won the princess by the power of the genie and eventually became a king. He didn't dream of a windfall from the beginning, but the magic power became his everything once he had the genie.

He didn't make a fortune by working, and he took over the throne without any political vision. Whenever he faces difficulties in the future, he will rely on the lamp genie.

Think about Job in the Bible. He praised the Lord even amid a disaster. Job 1:21 NLT says, "The Lord gave me what I had, and the Lord has taken it away. Praise the name of the Lord!"

Although everything was taken away, Job was able to praise God, which is the Christian faith. But what about Aladdin? What would be left to him if there is no genie?

1 Corinthians 10:31 says, "So whether you eat or drink or whatever you do, do it all for the glory of God."

Aladdin uses the genie's power to eat or drink, and he will never understand the life living for God's glory. Don't be envious of such a magical life.

Jesus says that if our focus is to expand His Kingdom, by sharing the Good News of His Salvation, then we don't have to worry about where our food comes from or any other material needs. He will provide. Matthew 6:33 – "But seek first his kingdom and his righteousness, and all these things will be given to you as well."

The difference is us doing God's will, not a genie doing our will.

For Christians, God's will is our only wish.

Memorable Quotes

*Reference Book: Andrew Lang. (Ed.) (1889). The Blue Fairy Book. (London: Longmans, Green & Co). *Aladdin and The Wonderful Lamp* was retrieved from https://etc.usf.edu/lit2go/141/the-blue-fairy-book/3132/aladdin-and-the-wonderful-lamp/

- ring genie

  For two days Aladdin remained in the dark, crying and lamenting. At last he clasped his hands in prayer, and in so doing rubbed the ring, which the magician had forgotten to take from him. Immediately an enormous and frightful genie rose out of the earth, saying: "What wouldst thou have with me? I am the Slave of the Ring, and will obey thee in all things." Aladdin fearlessly replied: "Deliver me from this place!" whereupon the earth opened, and he found himself outside.

- lamp genie

  As it was very dirty, she began to rub it, that it might fetch a higher price. Instantly a hideous genie appeared, and asked what she would have. She fainted away, but Aladdin, snatching the lamp, said boldly: "Fetch me something to eat!" The genie returned with a silver bowl, twelve silver plates containing rich meats, two silver cups, and two bottles of wine.

o   Master, I obey.

He rubbed it, and the genie appeared, saying, "What is thy will?" Aladdin replied: "The Sultan, as thou knowest, has broken his promise to me, and the Vizier's son is to have the Princess. My command is that tonight you bring hither the bride and bridegroom." "Master, I obey," said the genie.

About the Author

Regan Kim was born in Korea and immigrated to New Zealand in 2001. He is a novelist, essayist, and blogger belonging to NZ Christian Writers and the Korean Christian Writers Association.

His writings have been published mainly on blogs so far. For 7 years Regan has had an English blog titled *Worship through Novels* on Google and a Korean blog with the same title on Naver.

Christian Life, a Korean-language newspaper in NZ, published his three novels and forty-seven essays for five years.

Regan attends Hanouri Church in Auckland, NZ, and has completed the diploma course of theology at Coramdeo Theological Seminary.

Grace is his beloved wife and lifetime friend. He always thanks God for giving Joanne, John, and Dana as a family.

Looking at his two grandkids, Chloe and Roy, Regan dreams that many future Christians who love *Worship Through Novels* will shine beautifully like stars in the night sky.

Regan hopes that *Worship Through Novels* will serve as a helpful channel for readers to be the kind of worshipers the Father seeks. (John 4:23 NIV)